AS SAFE AS HOUSES

Ramblings About Real Estate
in Quote and Metaphor

Andrew Crosby

Aenspire Publishing

Published by Aenspire Publishing

Remuera, Auckland,

New Zealand

publishing@aenspire.com

© 2018 Andrew Crosby

This book is copyright. Except for the purpose of fair reviewing, no part of this publication may be reproduced or transmitted in any form or by any means, electronic or mechanical, including photocopying, recording, or any information storage and retrieval system, without permission in writing from the publisher. Infringers of copyright render themselves liable to prosecution.

While the publisher and author have used their best efforts in preparing this book, they make no representations or warranties with respect to the accuracy or completeness of the contents of this book and specifically disclaim any implied warranties of merchantability or fitness for a particular purpose. No warranty may be created or extended by sales representatives or written sales materials. The advice and strategies contained herein may not be suitable for your situation. You should consult with a professional where appropriate. Neither the publisher or author shall be liable for any loss of profit or other commercial damages, including but not limited to special, incidental, consequential or other damages.

This publication is brought to you by

www.developmentprofit.com

To Clare, Maximillian & Penelope

Dad:	"What's my job?"
Max (Age 7):	"I don't know, find properties to build houses?"
Dad:	"How do we build houses?"
Max:	"Get a plan and an architect."
Dad:	"What does the architect do?"
Max:	"Architect designs the house."
Dad:	"Then what do we do?"
Max:	"Find out where to build it. Then you find all the things you need, like bricks and concrete, then you build it."
Dad:	"And after that?
Max:	"Then you find an owner, by putting it on Trademe*. Once the owner has bid on it they come to where it's built and they live there."
Dad:	"Yep, that's pretty much it!!"

* Online auction website in New Zealand, like eBay.

Contents

Introduction 11

Chapter One Selling and the Market 15

Chapter Two Investment 29

Chapter Three Being a Contrarian 43

Chapter Four Development 57

Chapter Five Construction 79

Chapter Six Architecture 97

Chapter Seven Lifestyle 129

Chapter Eight Leadership 153

Epilogue 175

References 179

About the Author 199

Introduction

Property — the real estate kind — is analogous to so many different things. I often find myself creating quotes or metaphors to better describe some aspect of the property industry to peers and students. It is such a vibrant field, the mind tends to wander all over the place. In other books I start every chapter with a famous quote to metaphorically represent that subject. Through only a few words or ten, the best quotes can summarize an entire chapter by the richness of the thoughts they invoke.

The idea for this book came one day whilst I was on a business related social media website. I regularly post articles or links to stories or comment or even make requests to whomever is listening — typically having a

Introduction

property development related focus as that is my day (and night) job. One evening, in a flight of fancy, I decided to turn the lyrics of a classic song into a 'quote' to represent the declining real estate market in a particular location. On another occasion I created a short rhyming monologue to describe how I saw consultants getting greedy and not paying attention to who was paying the bills (me as developer!). Both posts received quite a number of comments and likes – many more than my other boring (but more informative) posts. That got me thinking I should document all my little sayings and whimsical verbal gestures, just in case some are any good (the jury is out!). That logically led to the thought, if I am going to bother documenting them, why not write a book!

In this self-indulgent literary exposé, I have selected what I think are the cleverest quotes from others and added my own fabrications arranged in various topics that underpin the real estate industry. Many quotes are from famous and successful property aficionados – the past and present billionaires of the industry. Where the link to real estate and property may not be so obvious, or the reason for including such a quote unclear, I occasionally attach my reinterpretation. For others, an interesting factoid or three is thrown in.

It's been fun to put this book together, a pleasant deviation from the more detailed non-fiction manuscripts I create or the hard grind of property development that occupies every weekday endeavour. Enjoy, and please excuse this idiosyncratic (and quite possibly simply nutty) endeavour.

Introduction

"Metaphorical language is a species of natural language which we construct out of arbitrary but concrete words. That is why it is so pleasing."

Georg Christoph Lichtenberg – Eighteenth century German philosopher and physicist, whose writings were often satirical and humorous.

Chapter One

Selling and the Market

The real estate market can be tough. In growth cities around the world, the market cycles in a five to ten year rotation. From a period of relative nothingness, the market begins to show signs of life, starts accelerating and then launches into rapid sales. Escalating house prices dominate breakfast conversations at corner cafés. At the peak every airport bound taxi driver is a real estate 'flipping' expert. Then the market sours. Transactions slow down and eventually it descends into a depression where property becomes a dirty word at dinner parties and failed developers line the business section of local newspapers.

Selling and the Market

The people doing the selling and leasing are an interesting bunch. Realtors and estate agents don't normally rate highly on the most trusted professionals published lists — often rounding out the bottom three with used car salesman and politicians. When the property market tide is in, tailored suits and German car sales flourish — paid for from the lucrative proceeds of colossal commissions. Unfortunately Pareto's 80/20 law applies and many agents fail to make a decent living, while the gifted (of the gab) few, get to enjoy the spoils. Those 20 percenters can survive the inevitable market trough and as the market fires up will be accompanied by a fresh batch of newbies eager to follow in their Italian leather footsteps.

As Safe as Houses

> "Don't blame the market,
> make the market."

Andrew Crosby [hereinafter AJC]

After a four year boom, buyers disappeared, pretty much overnight in Auckland. The key reason being banks had become extremely conservative in their lending due to the government implementing loan to value restrictions. This was a time of change where agents, softened by years of simply order-taking, needed to get back to the basics of hard selling.

Selling and the Market

> "To my real estate agent,
> Chernobyl is a fixer-upper."

Yakov Smirnoff – Soviet-American comedian.

Read through real estate listings enough times and you will see the same old cliché headlines and rather questionable claims accentuating anything remotely positive. For example, 'Renovators Dream' (a real dive), 'Low Maintenance' (no backyard) and 'Won't Last' (no one wants me).

As Safe as Houses

"A funny thing happens in real estate.
When it comes back,
it comes back up like gangbusters."

Barbara Corcoran – New York City real estate business entrepreneur, and columnist.

The market can appear to be going nowhere, and then all of a sudden it has a year or two of rapid price appreciation as demand soaks up existing space and new supply takes years to bring to market.

Selling and the Market

"In real estate you make 10% of your money because you're a genius and 90% because you catch a great wave."

Jeff Greene – Real estate investor and mogul who famously shorted subprime before the 2008 housing bubble collapse.

Luck has a lot to do with making short-term money in real estate. Of course you can create your own luck by buying and being in the market — just don't think you are an expert when all you are doing is floating on a rising tide.

As Safe as Houses

"That was a bloodbath, for a good reason. When the economy crashes or even really wavers, a terrible thing happens if you're in the real estate brokerage business. Buyers and sellers do nothing. Nothing is terrible for brokerage. A big seller's market is great because it's action. A horrible market is great because people have to sell. But in the beginning, when nothing happens, you go out of business."

Barbara Corcoran
In addition to real estate she was also a reality television show star on *Shark Tank* — where promising (or not so) entrepreneurs try to entice the sharks to invest in their venture.

Selling and the Market

"In today's real estate jungle,
vendors swing from the trees,
while buyers forage on the floor."

AJC

The post peak of a real estate market can result in dramatically opposing price expectations between buyers and sellers.

As Safe as Houses

"By 2003, every fool was getting into real estate. The checkout girl at my local supermarket handed me her newly printed real estate agent business card."

Robert Kiyosaki – Real estate investor and author of best-selling *Rich Dad Poor Dad*.

In Phoenix 2006 I (AJC) had two policemen come into my show home fully uniformed. I hesitantly asked if I could be of assistance, with thoughts going through my mind of what crime we had unwittingly committed or had fallen victim to. They replied, "Oh we're actually moonlighting weekend realtors looking to see what you have for sale."

Selling and the Market

"Property markets go up, down and sideways.
When it's going up and you're going sideways
you feel depressed
— because you feel you are missing out.

When it's going sideways or down
and you're going down
you feel depressed
— because you are losing money.

When it's going down and you're lucky
enough to be going sideways, or even up
everyone else around you will be depressed
— so you will still feel depressed."

AJC
Real estate decisions are often dominated by emotions, especially the feeling of missing out.

As Safe as Houses

"This is my strategy: not to negotiate.
That is negotiation."

Fredrik Eklund – Realtor star on *Million Dollar Listing New York*, a reality television show profiling the business antics of some of the Big Apple's most successful agents.

Selling and the Market

"The girls at *Hooters* look a lot better
during a housing recession.
When the boom was on,
the best looking ones were snapped up for
fancy new home and apartment showrooms.
With the boom over,
they all now serve chicken."

AJC

Actual observation over numerous chicken wing dinners, pre and post the global financial crisis, at *Hooters* restaurant downtown Phoenix, 2005 to 2010.

As Safe as Houses

"The best time to buy a home
is always five years ago."

Ray Brown – American jazz musician.
Think of the number of times you hear people say, 'I wish I had bought that house way back then…'

Selling and the Market

"Peak Agent."

AJC

The time in the cycle where the maximum number of agents or realtors are employed. My cynical predictor of a pending market decline. Also closely aligned to 'Peak Seminar' when not so scrupulous promoters tout their overpriced properties under the pretence of giving you an education in real estate investment.

Chapter Two

Investment

As safe as houses, they say. Investing in real estate has proven to be a significant wealth generator for many of the world's richest. Eventually, in a growing city, prices for residential and commercial property will appreciate and you should make money. Though how long you have to wait is one thing and how much you have to spend while you wait is another.

Investment to those in the industry is about buying at the price where there is sufficient cash-flow to pay your costs and cover the note/mortgage and generate a surplus for your back pocket. However, the word investment gets thoroughly abused in buoyant markets.

Investment

People confuse buying a home, renovating it and flipping it, an investment (that's speculation). Or, mistakenly, they consider a highly leveraged 'no money down deal' that loses money every month, hoping to reap a capital gain, an investment (that's gambling!).

As Safe as Houses

"Ninety percent of all millionaires
become so through owning real estate.
More money has been made in real estate
than in all industrial investments combined.
The wise young man or wage earner of today
invests his money in real estate."

Andrew Carnegie – Steel tycoon and one of the richest men in the nineteenth century.

Of course a million dollars doesn't buy you much in most growing cities anymore!

Investment

"The best time to invest in property is all the time,
if you know what you are doing."

Donald Trump – Forty-fifth President of the United States.

For my internet company public newsletter I asked the Don in 2003, "Why is the worst time the best time to invest in property?" He graciously replied on gold embossed letterhead with his distinctive handwritten signature. Here is another extract from his response:

"You also have to know where you're doing what. A sensational idea for New York might be a fizzle somewhere else. Its's absolutely necessary to know your market, and this requires constant research and attention on your part."

As Safe as Houses

"Location, location, location
is the default position only if you miss
timing, timing, timing."

AJC

I subsequently heard a very similar phrase coined by a developer on a podcast so possibly not my original. Location won't help you when there is a systemic market collapse — especially if you have overpaid for the privilege of that great location. A good location should bounce back quicker though.

Investment

"Don't wait to buy real estate.
Buy real estate and wait."

Will Rogers – Early twentieth century movie actor and social commentator.

Many investors have grown substantial retirement funds through the accumulation of properties that (eventually) appreciate, even if first purchased just before a downturn. Detroit is not a terribly good example.

As Safe as Houses

"We brought the worst house on the worst street.

Then we renovated: it became the

best house on the worst street.

Then we did nothing for ten years: it returned to the

worst house on the worst street.

So we did it up and sold it: as once again

the best house on the worst street.

AJC

In that case we were very passive investors with very destructive tenants. But with the passage of time and even after paying for two renovations we made a killing.

Investment

> "I can't read a computer screen
> and never use a calculator.
> It's all in my head and by hand."

Simon Reuben – A British real estate and metals mogul. Born in Mumbai, he and his brother David made a fortune investing in Russia's aluminium sector.

Prolific developers can instinctively pull together a financial feasibility in their heads in seconds — usually as accurate an indicator of profit as any spreadsheet.

As Safe as Houses

"Because everybody wants what everybody wants. And when there are ten buyers and only three puppies, every dog becomes the pick of the litter."

Barbara Corcoran – reciting her mother's astute words.

Supply and demand. In this analogy even the most unfavorable puppy will have a buyer. Similarly in real estate markets, growing demand will eventually soak up all supply, and in doing so cause prices to rise. Eventually prices rise so much that new supply (development) is profitable enough to start building and satisfy that demand.

Investment

"Real estate cannot be lost or stolen,
nor can it be carried away.
Purchased with common sense,
paid for in full,
and managed with reasonable care,
it is about the safest investment in the world."

Franklin D. Roosevelt – Thirty-second President of the United States, elected four times.

The 'paid for in full' part of this quote is sometimes forgotten by many — at times debt can make real estate an extremely unsafe investment.

As Safe as Houses

"When the market is booming

you want cash to grow.

When the market is busting

you need cash to flow."

AJC
On the importance of having cash flow to carry you (and your bank) through a downturn.

Investment

"The best investment on earth is earth."

Louis Glickman – New York real estate investor and philanthropist. Philharmonic devotees say his best deal was the one he never concluded — the purchase and demolition of famed Carnegie Hall to create an office building.

As Safe as Houses

"If you don't own a home buy one,
if you own one home, buy another one,
and if you own two homes buy a third
and lend your relatives the money to buy a home."

John Paulson – Investor and ultra-contrarian billionaire who bet against US subprime debt.

Here indirectly referring to the tax benefits and seemingly never-ending eventual appreciation (albeit often in a curvy line) of house prices.

Investment

"The major fortunes in America have been made in land."

John D. Rockefeller – Oil baron whose dynasty went on to develop the original Twin Towers, World Trade Center.

Chapter Three

Being a Contrarian

Money is made in real estate when you buy low and sell high. The problem is you can never predict at the time you are buying if it is low or if it is high! You can, of course, hazard an opinion about which way prices will go.

Asset bubbles form when almost everyone goes all-in, and unfortunately most people go all-in at precisely the peak. That includes previously vocal opponents, who ultimately psychologically capitulate. The few who go all-in during the depths of a recessionary trough are either lucky or clairvoyant.

To get this chapter started we borrow from Clem Chambers, contributing to Forbes.com (April 28, 2014), who put together a list on investment contrarianism.

Being a Contrarian

Forbes' Golden Rules of Contrarian Investing:
1. When you read about it in the newspapers or see it on the news, it is already all over.
2. Buy when everyone wants to sell and sell when everyone wants to buy.
3. No one sees a bubble when their income depends on it.
4. Don't take tips or advice and don't believe research notes.
5. What is obvious to you is not obvious to others.

As Safe as Houses

> "Following the herd is easy.
> At the time it just seems the only way to go.
> Going against the herd is difficult.
> There are a million self-doubt reasons
> why you wouldn't.
> That's why it is almost psychologically impossible
> to be a contrarian real estate investor."

AJC

Thinking you can predict the market is preposterous — still, many claim they can. Some argue by extrapolating a historical line, what the future will hold. The past, whilst contributing many lessons to be repeated — so you can at least be prepared — has proven it is no predictor of the future.

Being a Contrarian

"When everyone is going left,
look right."

Sam Zell – One of America's most prolific (billionaire) developers. In the mid-1980s real estate crash, he put his words into practice and acquired office and residential properties at fire-sale prices.

As Safe as Houses

> "That development is an oil painting on a wafer thin canvas. It won't take much to break the pretty picture."

AJC

Describing a government housing development that had a very low percentage of public housing and was presented immaculate to private home buyers. However, with a deteriorating private sales market there is the potential for political decision makers to offset poor sales by requiring much higher numbers of public housing. If not managed carefully this could increase crime via the presence of local gangs and the subdivision could easily devolve into the next generation's ghetto. Let's hope they get it right!

Being a Contrarian

"New Yorkers are predatory about real estate.
When they sense softening,
they move in for the kill."

Anderson Cooper – American journalist and television presenter at CNN.

Many recognize New York as being at the top of the international real estate pyramid (no Ponzi scheme implied!), and also one of the most competitive.

As Safe as Houses

"You only find out who is swimming naked when the tide goes out."

Warren Buffet – The legend of investing, occasionally in real estate companies.

This is another way of saying when the market turns, those who are laden with debt are most vulnerable to losing their shirt (and pants).

Being a Contrarian

"When there is blood on the streets,
buy in those streets."

AJC
My adaptation on the well-known quote.

As Safe as Houses

"I was dancing on the skeletons
of other people's mistakes."

Sam Zell

From a 1978 *Real Estate Review* article where he referred to being a real estate 'grave dancer', picking over the bones of failed projects.

There is a term in real estate development financing 'loan to own' where the financier doesn't mind ending up as the owner. Often the loans are at such exorbitant rates and fees that the (desperate) developer has no choice other than to fulfil the financier's prophecy.

Being a Contrarian

"Investors are notorious for treating recessions
as a permanent state of affairs,
thus missing opportunities and, conversely,
behaving recklessly in economic booms,
ignoring that they never last.
Successful investors are always counter-cyclical,
buying in gloom and selling in the inevitable boom."

Sir Bob Jones – New Zealand hard hitting occasional columnist and property investment mogul. His company, Robert Jones Holdings, formed in 1961, owns commercial property in New Zealand, Australia and the United Kingdom.

As Safe as Houses

> "A simple rule dictates my buying:
> Be fearful when others are greedy,
> and be greedy when others are fearful."

Warren Buffet

The peak of any market seemingly occurs just prior to the peak of greed. At that point an inevitable ethical collapse begins where those less scrupulous try to hold onto their paper wealth through whatever deceptive means necessary — often perpetuating the myth that the market will keep going up, when it is already going down.

Being a Contrarian

"Housing New Zealand is ideally placed to be the perfect contrarian developer and investor. They never ever have enough homes. When the market is booming the development department should shut up shop and wait it out. When the market softens and no one wants to buy then HNZ should buy everything they can afford.

This will help soften the falls in the property market, whilst allowing tax payer dollars to achieve some bargains. When all suitable surplus housing is absorbed, and assuming the market has now flattened or even crashed, then HNZ should fire up the development department and start building in earnest.

Short-term valuations should be ignored as it will all be worth more in ten years' time. This countercyclical investment will provide employment to builders and consultants in tough times as well as ensure the government is building at the cheapest possible rates."

AJC
A philosophical but practically difficult to achieve conclusion reached after four years working at the government housing department.

As Safe as Houses

"There's usually a 10-year cycle,
but people have eight-year memories."

Rick Caruso – An American retail mega developer and billionaire. His flagship center being The Grove in L.A.

Chapter Four

Development

Buying land, obtaining planning approval, selling and then building can be a lucrative business. Real estate development is also very risky. The number of variables outside your control is mind boggling. Even with rising property prices you can come unstuck. Much has been quoted on just how painful the process can be.

Yes, development has been my gig for almost two decades now. I have been through bull, flat, bad and inconceivably horrid bear markets. Persistence and not accepting anything (that doesn't help your project) are two traits a successful developer needs to master. Outright positivity is also the main reason why anything

Development

ever gets built. If you looked at development logically and comprehensively, usually the risks routinely outweigh the rewards. No one sensible would do it and very little would ever get built. However, thankfully, there are always those ready to dive in and take a punt on their abilities – the lure of a tremendous fortune on paper is just too great. Realizing that fortune and keeping it is another matter!

Property developers don't get a good rap in movies, often portrayed as the villain destroying (gentrifying) a neighborhood. But without them the world would be a much duller place. The skyscrapers of New York, the man-made islands in Dubai, the suburbs your parents lived in (OK, that may be a poor example) all had developers behind them. In every case, to make the project happen, they were the ones who ran the show — often a stress-brimmed concoction of action, endurance, tenacity, deal hammering and self-preservation, plus sweet talking a bank or two!

As Safe as Houses

"Property development can be like a Masterchef challenge. You set out to bake a gourmet chocolate gateau although the judges don't allow you to have the full recipe. Another contestant places salt in the sugar jar, not maliciously but simply forgets to inform. The stove mysteriously stops half way through and when you call the supplier they are all on a training course. Five hours into a supposed two hour cook time, you are just happy to present an undercooked sponge with salted caramel icing and hope no one gets sick when they finally eat it."

AJC

Anyone who has done development understands what I mean. Think of the bureaucratic subjective city planning authority as the *judges*, a junior consulting engineer as a *contestant* and a building contractor running away from their contractual obligations as the *supplier*.

Development

"The developing world has an opportunity to join with our house-building friends to build communities that reflect the age we live in rather than the past. We live in the age of Google and iPod; we build in the age of Romans."

Sir Stuart Lipton – A British developer responsible for over 20 million square feet of development in London. He has been referred to as 'the king of big projects', with London's Silverton regeneration his latest: a 3.5 billion pound project for 3,000 homes, office and various dining and retail outlets.

As Safe as Houses

"The knife of a failed property development
project is very sharp and jagged.
If you do decide to catch it,
make sure you have on your best protective gloves."

AJC

Taking on a failed project, even if it looks like a bargain, will not be easy, because it often has fundamental issues — many of which you will not discover until much later. The key is to not overpay for hidden risks. Also question your self-belief that you are any better than the last developer. Was it him or the project that was really the problem?

Development

"We used to call them our 'town founders' and we honored them by erecting their statues in our town squares. Today we just call them developers."

Andrés Duany – An American architect, urban planner and a founder of the Congress for the New Urbanism.

Worse, developers are often portrayed as the bad guy both in the movies and by the media.

As Safe as Houses

"When the heroin ran out,
the junkie moved to property development"

AJC

Adrenaline pumping, addictive and highly risky, developers tend to lust for more: bigger and bolder projects. Unfortunately, many times it is that last final mega project 'hit' that is their downfall. Bankruptcy then becomes their rehab.

Development

"Any damn fool can build homes.
What counts is how many you can sell for how little."

William Levitt – Creator of Levittown in 1947 and an estimated 140,000 houses over his career. Urban historian Kenneth T. Jackson said that the Levitt family had the greatest impact on post war housing in the United States.

If you pack your projects full of features that your target market is not prepared to pay for, then spiraling costs can quickly quash any profit.

As Safe as Houses

"Property development is somewhat akin
to painting a modern masterpiece.
It requires arranging various elements
into a collective composition that works
successfully as a whole.
However, as many a painter can attest to,
often these works of art are the result of
constant modification and repainting.
Where the artist ends up, whilst a triumph of
realising their vision in paint, is often not
what was originally envisaged."

AJC
Here I go again, saying essentially the same thing. The gist is development can take many twists and turns.

Development

"Every developer, as you grow,
wants to do things that are transformative
and have a real impact on the city
that you're working with."

Stephen M. Ross – Chairman of Related, the company behind America's largest private development, Hudson Yards in Manhattan, New York.

As Safe as Houses

> "Success in development
> isn't about creative buildings,
> it's about creative finance."

AJC

Creative financing structures can get your development project started, keep it going and save you (or at least prolong the agony) at the end. Funding is your friend but time is your enemy. There are three reasons developers are in a race against time: 1) the interest you have to pay on debt, 2) a sales or leasing market changing for the negative, and 3) increasing construction costs.

Development

"If you look at real estate developments, especially for one company, you need to excel in every city that you go to and you need to make sure that you have depth, because it takes a lot to build a new set up in every new city, to learn the laws, to understand how to get your permits, to seek contractors and consultants and architects. Then you have to understand the banking sector. To enter a new country with only one project is not financially viable."

Ziad El Chaar – Managing Director Damac Properties, a Dubai listed developer with billion dollar plus annual revenues, on why being the biggest in the world doesn't mean being all over the world.

There is a lot to get up to speed on when entering a new market. My theory is when the foreigners enter town, it's time to get out of the development game. Having been a foreigner starting developments, merely months before the peak (and a dramatic decline), may have colored my opinion of course!

As Safe as Houses

"A developer who is not optimistic shouldn't be a developer."

Harry Triguboff

Or as the Sydney media like to refer to him, 'High rise Harry'. His company Meriton has built more than 70,000 apartments.

Development

"Look for opportunities in markets
with pent-up demand."

Sam Zell

Also author of the book *Am I Being Too Subtle?* and reported to tell the Wall Street Journal in 1985, "If it ain't fun, we don't do it."

In his quote above, pent-up demand is difficult to find as you don't really know that market exists until you actually supply to it (and that takes guts and costs money). Sam is an expert at solving such enigmas.

As Safe as Houses

"Three things you need to be a property developer:

Left ball, right ball, other people's money."

AJC
At least applicable to many entrepreneurial private developer types.

Development

"I'm a third-generation builder.

I enjoy what I'm doing.

If somebody asked me, 'What's your favorite deal?'

I'd say it's the next one I'm doing…"

Geoff Palmer – One of the most successful housing developers in Los Angeles. Worth an estimated $3 billion, in 2015 Eddie Kim of Los Angeles Downtown News described Palmer as both the "most prolific" and "most controversial" developer in downtown L.A.

As Safe as Houses

"When the morning radio music stops,
all consultants should remember this:
without developers there are no new buildings.
With no new buildings there is
no need for building consultants.
No need for consultants means no developers'
money for consultants to pay for their breakfast toast.
Developers take risks to get buildings built.
Yes, there are rewards, but often it takes a
12 child family at breakfast juggling act.
If you are a consultant and were around in 2010,
you know how hard it was to pay for the toast.
While you are pouring on the jam at the moment,
please don't burn the toast."

AJC
A blatant social media warning to consultants getting lazy with their developer clients — times are good now but they won't always be. Arrogance, especially in some engineers, seems to build with workload and fee generation.

Development

*"There's one stockholder and that's me.
To do something crazy,
you have to do it alone."*

Carvalho Hosken – Billionaire Brazilian developer and a prime beneficiary of public infrastructure spending for the Rio Olympic games. He had land holdings equivalent to 8,000 football pitches in and around the main Olympic site.

As Safe as Houses

"It's a war out there.
I should write a book about it."
AJC vents in an email.

Bank manager replies,
"Yes it'll be a drama!"

AJC & Unnamed Bank Manager
Recent dialogue referring to the time spent (months) with local authorities at gaining the final sign-off on a subdivision.

Development

"I am infected with an incurable malady
called developers' disease.
I build first and ask questions later."

Steve Wynn – Flamboyant Las Vegas and Macau casino magnate. Earlier involved in the re-development of the *Golden Nugget*, and later the *Bellagio* and, of course, his very own *Wynn*.

As Safe as Houses

"Display suites are developer porn."

AJC

Yes, I like visiting new cities, going to new restaurants, taking in the sights, experiencing new cultures. But what I like best (and typically when my wife goes shopping) is visiting all the new development project marketing displays and showrooms.

Development

"I tried all my life to make housing affordable.
The more affordable the house,
the more money I make."

Harry Triguboff

In any residential market, squeezing the maximum number of homes/units on a site, at the smallest unit size that market will absorb, and at the most economical construction quality that market expects, is generally the most profitable approach.

Chapter Five

Construction

Delivering buildings is not for the faint-hearted, the unprepared or those who throw caution to the wind. It is the construction phase where the developer goes *all-in* with their (or least their bank's) money — the delivery of a physically sound and occupant friendly structure their ultimate aim. All too often the developer or the contractor doesn't come out with any money. The build is where an architect's fantastical creation on paper meets the cold, hard reality of concrete, steel, wood, regulations, bureaucracy, buildability and cost efficiency. The dream sometimes metamorphosed into a collage of lost opportunity. For those careful enough to set lofty goals, manage

Construction

expectations, be blessed with a cash rich benefactor and afforded the will to innovate, construction can result in a step forward for mankind.

Construction is run by very practical types. Contractors and subcontractors, manufacturers and suppliers – these are the people who build and make and sell the stuff that goes into a building. Between them, the architect, the engineer and the developer are volumes of documents and legal contracts. That's where things can get messy. Real messy. When a problem arises and once emotions have vented, 'lawyer up' is often the reaction. Every (wo)man , upon their insurer's advice, flees to their respective corner, gloves up and engages in the battle game of blame.

As Safe as Houses

"We shape our buildings thereafter they shape us."

Sir Winston Churchill – World War II United Kingdom Prime Minister. In October 2016, his old home (the one he died in) and carrying the prestigious address 28 Hyde Park Gate, was for sale for the paltry sum of £22,900,000.

Construction

"You can't build a great building on a weak foundation. You must have a solid foundation if you're going to have a strong superstructure."

Gordon B. Hinckley – American religious leader.

The metaphor applies to so much in real estate. Not only to physical construction, but also to your sales and marketing strategy, and especially the fine print of deals made when plunging into contract.

As Safe as Houses

"If you owe the bank $100
that's your problem.
If you owe the bank $100 million,
that's the bank's problem."

J. Paul Getty – Oil baron and the subject of a biography *The Richest American* by Ralph Hewins, published in 1960. *Fortune* magazine asked him about his wealth in 1957 in which he famously countered, "But, remember, a billion dollars isn't worth what it used to be."

Construction

"Humans have been building houses for 3000 years.
So why only in the last 20 have we
managed to make them leak?"

AJC
Bar time expression in response to New Zealand's leaky building crisis.

As Safe as Houses

"How come the shortest distance between two points is always under construction?"

Unknown Writer – at *Changing Times, The Kiplinger Magazine*, 1966.

In construction, there are always those seeking the industry to be more productive, with the prefabrication faithful at the top of the heap.

Construction

"Nothing is built on stone;

all is built on sand,

but we must build as if the sand were stone."

Jorge Luis Borges – Argentine poet, essayist, and short-story writer (quote from *In Praise of Darkness*, 1974).

My simple comprehension of Jorge's comment is that regardless of never-ending change, you must put a line in the sand (to extend the cliché) and simply get on with it — design it, build it, develop it.

As Safe as Houses

"Even the three little pigs started with stick,
but ended with brick."

AJC
On the sellable merits of the simple, but effective, economical and timeless brick and tile construction (a New Zealand thing).

Construction

"As the builders say,
the larger stones do not lie well without the lesser."

Plato – The student of Socrates and the teacher of Aristotle — so even he was in fairly good company!

Think of a stone wall; you need the small stones to fill in the gaps and hold up the larger ones. The small stones representing the detail in construction documents, for example. When the detail is not correct, the large stones will fall down and the wall will crumble.

As Safe as Houses

"If you have to read the contract small print then it's already too late."

Unnamed Builder

A conversation I had in relation to a construction contract: if it comes down to having to go through the legal small print to resolve (assign blame) an issue then that is a symptomatic sign of builder-developer relationship (and project) in trouble. In this particular case we just sorted it out and split the difference — no point feeding the lawyers.

Construction

> "When we build,
> let us think that we build forever."

John Ruskin – Nineteenth century English sage and critic of art, architecture, and society.

Build to last is a worthy goal but with advancing technology, and changing lifestyles and work habits (driven by things such as remote access and transport), functional obsolescence, before the buildings physical use-by date, must be acknowledged. Many now design for adaptive re-use potential.

As Safe as Houses

"There are two types of contractors:
those who price jobs, and
those who buy jobs."

AJC
Remark concerning the age-old practice of builders who quote low prices to win the job and try to make up their shortfall on variations during the contract. When the developer is on their game and protects (via contracts and good documentation) their risk away, time after time builders end up bankrupt.

Construction

"When one has finished building one's house,
one suddenly realizes that in the process
one has learned something that
one really needed to know in the worst way
— before one began."

Friedrich Nietzsche – German philosopher and cultural critic intensively active in the 1870s and 1880s.

For many who have built their own home, without prior experience in the construction industry, comes the harsh reality of budget overruns and delays — mainly forged from their own doing. In retrospect it was all so obvious!

As Safe as Houses

"We have become so quick and effective in building things today…I'm afraid what we are building today will not have the same impact and sustainability of the architecture of a 100, 500 or 1,000 years ago. The buildings of those days were miracles. We don't perform such miracles today."

Zhang Xin – CEO of SOHO China, she is also known as the 'woman who built Beijing', responsible for developing over 55 million square feet in Beijing and Shanghai.

Construction

"Prefabrication is a fabrication."

AJC

The faster, cheaper and more efficient way to build a house through 'prefab' remains elusive. Making prefab work requires industry buy-in, repetition and consistency. These are notoriously difficult to achieve because the industry is slow (with little vested interest) to change, every house has a unique site, and the market always inconsistently cycles through production demand peaks and troughs.

As Safe as Houses

"The essence of engineering
consists not so much in the mere construction
of the spectacular layouts or developments,
but in the invention required
—the analysis of the problem,
the design,
the solution by the mind which directs it all."

William Hood – Chief Engineer of the Southern Pacific (California) Railroad.

Hmm, I wish all engineers adhered to Mr Hood's dedication to finding great (cost-effective, aesthetic and reliable) engineering solutions.

Chapter Six
Architecture

Architects, designers, engineers, developers, builders, planners, urban designers and officials all contribute to the creation of architecture. Inspirational, generation defining, fairly average, or just simply grotesque — in the eye of the beholder — architecture can result.

I often think of the architectural profession as one of the most frustrating (and I trained as one, so have a little insider knowledge). A building commences with a vision and a dream. From deep within their intellectual sanctuary the architect masters their imagination to create something awe-inspiring. They savor a few weeks of embracing their conceptual pièce de résistance. In

Architecture

their hearts they feel that this will be a sublime creation, a building that will transcend its mere physical presence and will enter the academic architectural lexicon for design students to be inspired for decades to come. Bang! The costs have just come in and they are not pretty. With a swoop of the developer's eraser, a quarter of the cost and half the architect's ingenious embellishments disappear. Smack! The council bureaucracy are now involved and the 'you can't do that' rhetoric destroys much of the architect's flair that remains. For months thereafter, architecture is a tedious process of drawing details, specifying materials, finding compromises, delivering technical solutions and the endless production of documentation. From there a soul destroying process, taking months or sometimes years of form filling, meetings, reviews, public consultation and back and forth with officials to obtain planning consent. Then when under construction, the architect can enjoy a myriad of contractor requests mainly relating to problems that were not adequately considered in design, disputes and further design versus cost compromises. Finally, the building is complete and the architect manages to find a few angles to photograph that give the illusion of a masterpiece to include in their portfolio. However, the fun never really stops as over the next few years (or ten), the architect strives to keep their head down, avoiding any passing glint in the eye of defect claim litigators.

Poor architects, it really is full credit to those professionals who can execute memorable buildings they, their clients and the public can be proud of.

Architecture

"Each project, I suffer like
I'm starting over again in life.
There's a lot of healthy insecurity
that fuels this stuff."

Frank Gehry – Canadian-American celebrity architect, famous for architecture that flirts with abstract post-modernism. Works include the Guggenheim museum in Bilbao, and the Stata Center at MIT — a building he was later sued by MIT given its weather-tightness defects.

As Safe as Houses

"Less is more."

Peter Behrens (phrase originator, but the phrase later inextricably linked to **Ludwig Mies van der Rohe**) – Mies was an iconic pioneering modern architect and furniture designer. Born in Germany and last director of the Bauhaus, he moved to Chicago before WWII, serving as head of Illinois Institute of Technology's Department of Architecture and later designing many private office and apartment buildings. The Barcelona chair being probably his most famous furniture design.

Architecture

"MADNESS

=

My Architect Did Not Exactly Seek Savings."

AJC
Not infrequently, dreams come crashing down to reality when the build costs come in. A word of warning, don't leave it to your architect to provide costings!

As Safe as Houses

"Architecture is the art of how to waste space."

Philip Johnson – Prolific designer, winner of the prestigious Pritzker architecture prize and modernist master. The exemplary 1949 *Glass House* in Connecticut is his most well-known design.

Architecture

"Architecture should speak
of its time and place
but yearn for timelessness."

Frank Gehry

The Guardian reported that at a 2014 press conference in Oviedo, when asked if his architecture was just about spectacle, Gehry gave the journalist the finger. He then went on to say, "In this world we are living in, 98% of everything that is built and designed today is pure shit. There's no sense of design, no respect for humanity or for anything else. They are damn buildings and that's it."

As Safe as Houses

"The physician can bury his mistakes but an architect can only advise his clients to plant vines."

Frank Lloyd Wright – One of the world's most influential architects and educators, he established the distinctly American *Prairie School* style design. He founded the Taliesin Fellowship architecture school in Wisconsin with a winter studio and residence for architects that eventually became the exclusive Taliesin West, Frank Lloyd Wright School of Architecture in Arizona. Quintessential projects include the New York Guggenheim museum, and Falling Water, a Pennsylvanian residence integrated into an existing river and waterfall.

Architecture

"Where can we find greater structural clarity
than in the wooden buildings of the old?
Where else can we find such unity of material,
construction and form?
Here the wisdom of whole generations is stored."

Ludwig Mies van der Rohe
The story goes he got his first job in an architecture studio after working out — in just one hour — a drawing of a facade that his boss had been trying to resolve for weeks.

As Safe as Houses

"If I had to say what is my biggest contribution to the practice of architecture, I would say it is the achievement of hand-to-eye coordination."

"I think that is my best skill as an architect. I am able to transfer a sketch into a model into the building."

Frank Gehry

Many times what appears on architectural plans and is presented in computer generated photorealistic renders does not translate so attractively when it is actually built.

Architecture

"The first principle of architectural beauty
is that the essential lines of a construction
be determined by a perfect appropriateness to its use."

Gustave Eiffel – Given near free rein to design the most notable Parisian icon. Less commonly known is that the engineer was responsible for hundreds of metal structures around the world, including the structure within the Statue of Liberty and the locks of the Panama Canal.

As Safe as Houses

> "Trees, shrubs and vines
> grow a lost faster
> in renders than in reality."

AJC
Sometimes architects and developers just get it so wrong. What looked great in a computer generated sales render can fail on the aesthetic front so inordinately when built.

Architecture

"The life of a designer is a life of fight.
Fight against the ugliness.
Just like a doctor fights against disease.
For us, the visual disease is what we have around,
and what we try to do is cure it somehow,
you know, with design."

Massimo Vignelli – Italian architect and designer covering almost every conceivable form of design, including producing the New York subway map.

As Safe as Houses

"A great building must, in my opinion,
begin with the unmeasurable,
must go through the measurable
in the process of design,
but must again in the end be unmeasurable."

Louis Kahn – American era-defining modernist architect. One of his most acclaimed projects being the Sher-e-Bangla Nagar, government capital complex in Dhaka, Bangladesh.

OK, this most philosophical of architecture quotes is on a level higher than my pay grade, so I will take it down a notch: "Measure twice and cut once!"

Architecture

"To provide meaningful architecture
is not to parody history,
but to articulate it."

Daniel Libeskind – American architect whose designs include some striking angled additions to existing traditional edifices, including the Jewish Museum in Berlin and the Denver Art Museum. His deconstructive style of postmodern architecture is characterized by fragmentation and distortion (hence a lot of angled renovations).

As Safe as Houses

"Architecture is the will of the epoch translated into space."

Ludwig Mies van de Rohe
I translate this to architecture reflects the time, the will of the people in that time and all the other pressures and influences of the time. Mies should know, effectively the Bauhaus and modernism in Germany was shut down by the Nazi Gestapo and Hitler's amateur hour, closet architect inclinations.

Architecture

"The pen(cil) is mightier than the mouse."

AJC

Architects lose creativity when they design straight from the computer. They don't spend the time conceptualising space and form through the visceral act of sketching. Pencilmanship is dying out as architectural graduates default to the computer to even start off their designs. Will there ever be another like Barcelonan Antoni Gaudí with his monumental organic creations, conceived from the mind, not the computer? His church *Sagrada Familia*, still being built almost 100 years after his death, is a must visit.

As Safe as Houses

"Architecture is part of the politeia.

It is a political act;

it is not a private one…

One has to remember that the city is not only

built out of stone, glass, and concrete.

It is built out of its inhabitants

- the citizens who are really the substance of the city,

not simply the walls and spaces of the city."

Daniel Libeskind

Often though the cities' inhabitants can frustrate the delivery of great architecture. NIMBYism (Not In My Back Yard) refers to those vocal advocates for urban progress so long as it happens nowhere near them.

Architecture

"Design is where science and art break even."

Mieke Gerritzen – Dutch designer and published author on design.

In developer dialect: "Design is where *cost* and art break even!"

As Safe as Houses

"The desire to reach for the sky
runs very deep in the human psyche."

César Pelli — Argentine architect who became Dean at Yale School of Architecture and known for the Petronas Towers in Kuala Lumpur (the world's tallest building from 1998 to 2004).

Architecture

"Ultimately, architecture is all about well-being
– the creation of pleasant and stimulating
settings for all aspects of life
– but it is also important to build projects that give
uplifting experiences that inspire, excite and enthuse."

Zaha Hadid – Iraqi born, studied architecture in England and the first female winner of the Pritzker prize. Renowned for aesthetically inspiring works around the world, including the Riverside Museum in Glasgow and One Thousand Museum (condominiums) in Miami.

As Safe as Houses

"I call architecture frozen music."

Johann Wolfgang von Goethe – Eighteenth century writer, poet and statesman considered by many as the greatest German literary figure of the modern era.

Like music, good architecture can be subjective.

Architecture

"ARCHITECT, n.
One who drafts a plan of your house,
and plans a draft of your money;
who estimates the whole cost,
and himself costs the whole estimate."

Ambrose Bierce – Nicknamed 'bitter Bierce', an American Civil War solider and satirist authored *The Devil's Dictionary* (1911), named as one of the 100 greatest masterpieces of American literature. This quote is from that book's predecessor, *The Cynics Word Book* (1906).

As Safe as Houses

"As an architect you design for the present,
with an awareness of the past,
for a future which is essentially unknown."

Norman Foster – Baron Foster of Thames Bank – British 'starchitect', responsible for the Gherkin building in London.

What the future holds as far as functional obsolescence is impossible to predict. So is political interference. One apartment building I worked on renovating was originally designed to house working families just after the Second World War. The day before it opened, with a new government in charge, it was determined only to house the most needy, non-working, deprived, drug dependant and homeless. A few design changes necessary to protect residents from each other over the next 60 years wouldn't have gone amiss if that change could have been predicted.

Architecture

"I don't know why people hire architects
and then tell them what to do."

Frank Gehry

Most developers end up doing precisely this. An architect without a sense of build cost or practical engineering can tend to go on design tangents, embellishing the beautiful but financially unobtainable – at the developer's expense.

As Safe as Houses

"Architecture is the triumph of human imagination
over materials, methods, and men,
to put man into possession of his own Earth.

It is at least the geometric pattern of things,
of life, of the human and social world.

It is at best that magic framework of reality
that we sometimes touch upon
when we use the word 'order'."

Frank Lloyd Wright

Some critique FLW as having designs that don't actually work that well, but he was an experimentalist, and if you ever get the chance you need to visit Taliesin West in Scottsdale, Arizona to really understand his genius. The Biltmore Hotel (FLW inspired, designed by one of his students Albert Chase McArthur) is also worthy of a site/night inspection. I lived there for a couple of months so can personally guarantee you won't be disappointed.

Architecture

"David vs Goliath.

Developer vs Gareth at the Council."

AJC

The patriarch of even the most magnificent design still bears the burden of defeating the bureaucrat, with his long list of boxes to tick, on its journey to approval.

As Safe as Houses

"A house is a machine for living in."

Le Corbusier – One of the first names a student will see in their day one architectural history lecture — and will be referred to countless times before they graduate. Charles-Edouard Jeanneret-Gris was a Swiss born French architect and theorist with no less than 17 buildings on *UNESCO's World Heritage List*. His work and ideas have been influential on every architect. The *Church of Notre-Dame-du-Haut*, Ronchamp, and *Villa Savoye* in Poissy, both compete for the most published photographs of his architecture (and possibly any architects, ever).

Architecture

"I think being an architect and doing different
things is like the muscles in your body,
you have to train the different muscles
— the small ones and the big ones
— so that you remain flexible and active.
If you just do the same thing you become an expert
and a specialist, and you become blind."

Jacques Herzog — Of the famed Herzog & de Meuron Swiss architectural practice, a Pritzker prize winner with projects including the National Stadium (home of the 2008 Beijing Olympics), and London's Tate Museum's modern addition.

As Safe as Houses

"Architecture begins where engineering ends."

Walter Gropius – Another German pre-WWII exile to the United States, he founded the acclaimed *Bauhaus* in 1919 that was supremely important to the progression of modernist architecture.

Chapter Seven

Lifestyle

Playboy style parties — second only to James Bond — multiple divorces, The Robb Report, Gucci, Bugatti, Lamborghini, Audi (whatever else ending in the sound 'ee'). Along with their photos gracing the pages of gossip magazines, these are the hallmarks for better or worse of the world's real estate entrepreneurs.

In this high stakes, high risk, *Casino Royale* of built form industries, much of what you see is a carefully concocted illusion. The mantra being you have to look rich to get rich (or at least to get invited to the best parties in town). Those who are truly well heeled often despise notoriety and just get on with making money in relative

Lifestyle

obscurity, amassing great fortunes over generations and gifting much of it to worthy causes.

There is a lot of money in real estate. That can breed both flamboyance with extravagant lifestyles and the philanthropic — sometimes the same person with the latter a more mature reincarnation of the former.

As Safe as Houses

"I would like an island,
but I don't know what I would do with an island,
so I don't buy an island.
Everybody needs a home.
Not everybody needs an island."

Joseph Segal – Canadian billionaire developer, still working hard aged 92 at time of writing. His financial ability to buy an island formed decades ago when he founded a chain of discount department stores. He entered the real estate market with a simple philosophy: "The market is always a function of supply and demand. Too much supply, no demand, it tanks. Too much demand and no supply, it shoots way up."

Lifestyle

"I do not spend much on myself.
I give away every year seven or eight times as much
as I spend for personal comforts and pleasures."

Andrew Carnegie

Sold his company to JP Morgan for $480 million and went on to give away $350 million. A devotee of education, when public libraries were few and far between, in 1881 he went on to help fund the building of 2,509 libraries around the world.

As Safe as Houses

"Giving away money to the right cause,
with a leveraged effect
and your own involvement in how it is spent,
will 'give you peace of mind'."

Lee Shau Kee – Hong Kong based property developer with a $20 billion plus fortune in 2017. He gifted his staff $15 million in cash on the birth of his seventh grandchild.

Lifestyle

"I am not a person who pursues luxury.
I am not like those people who,
once they have money,
compulsively squander it or show it off."

Wang Jianlin — Another multi-billionaire real estate developer and one of China's wealthiest. His company is also the world's largest cinema operator.

As Safe as Houses

"I get great satisfaction from both business and philanthropy."

Donald Bren – Currently America's richest real estate developer, his Irvine Company literally created the city Irvine, California.

Lifestyle

"I could never read the American developers.
You could be sitting at a meeting with two: one dressed
in shorts, the other in an expensive suit. Both are talking
about their extensive portfolios,
high class lifestyles and their last private jet ride.

They both sounded equally full of it.

Only much later would you find out
one had no money and hired the suit to meet you,
while the other (in shorts) actually owned
a company that makes jets!"

AJC
Pretty close to a true story. My cynical summation after having many meetings with American real estate business people, and I could just never figure out where reality lay.

As Safe as Houses

"I don't know what London's coming to
— the higher the buildings the lower the morals."

Sir Noel Coward — A mid-twentieth century British playwright, actor, director, film producer, painter, songwriter, cabaret artist and writer. Nicknamed by close friends as 'The Master'.

Lifestyle

"For those already successful,
money can become a controlling factor in life
and make you a slave to it.
One way to avoid that – Philanthropy."

Lee Shau Kee
Nicknamed Asia's 'Master of Stock' for his share investment exploits. Donating sites (land) is one of his current philanthropies — two examples being one for a youth hostel and one for a nursing home (Asia's largest).

As Safe as Houses

"Private jets are really very polluting
so now I only have three."

Zhang Yue – CEO, Broad Group. Known as China's flat-pack skyscraper tycoon, in 2011 he erected a 30-story building in 15 days. In 2013 he was set to build his 202-story *Sky City*, in only seven months. As of writing it had yet to start construction, the officials seemingly hesitant to grant consent given the risk of innovation present in what would be the world's tallest building.

Lifestyle

"The ironic thing about possession

is that you don't possess the possessions,

the possessions possess you."

Philip Ng – With brother Robert and son of Ng Teng, who was affectionately called 'The King of Orchard Road', he is a multi-billionaire and Singapore's largest real estate developer.

As Safe as Houses

"I'm not going to hide my wealth,
I don't know why I should.
I've worked hard for this.
I wasn't born with a silver shoe,
so why not flash it?

You have the opportunity to do
what you want, when you want.
If you've got the balls,
nothing can stop you."

Danny Lambo – British property playboy.
Jon Lockett, journalist, comments on Danny in the *Sun* Newspaper: "Today his three hotels and property empire allow him to live a luxury lifestyle jetting around the world, buying cars from rappers such as 50 Cent and treating his many female friends to the finer things in life."

Lifestyle

"One of Beijing's top property developers has being [sic] charged with weapons offences after a late-night car race with another real estate mogul's son ended in flames and a heated row between the two notorious playboys.

Wang Ke and Wang Shuo were allegedly racing their cars on the streets of Beijing's popular shopping district Wangfujing in December when they both crashed near a busy intersection."

Clifford Coonan – Journalist reporting the story on 'the four capital playboys' — an elite group of young property developers from rich families, with money to burn, time to kill, film star girlfriends and a sense of entitlement that drives Beijingers crazy.

As Safe as Houses

"Prosecutors allege investors' money was not used for the purchase of real property but went to fund De Guzman's business and lavish lifestyle. Investor money was allegedly used to purchase a $1.8 million home, a $365,000 diamond ring, a $600,000 yacht, a $250,000 suite at Qwest Field for Seahawks games and a $200,000 Bentley automobile."

Levi Pulkkinen – Seattle journalist reporting the story on Jose L. Nino De Guzman Jr., 28, who sold 160 investors on real estate opportunities in Peru only to spend the money on his lifestyle.

There are so many shysters in the real estate industry and I have seen my fair share. Unfortunately the same old incredulous schemes keep reappearing every real estate cycle.

Lifestyle

"Fake it till you make it."

Unknown Origin

Well-worn philosophy by many in the real estate industry. Certainly helps the leased European luxury car industry make money!

As Safe as Houses

"A high-rolling lifestyle of fast cars, helicopters, penthouse apartments and VIP casino membership has caused an Auckland property developer to be convicted for contributing to his own bankruptcy.

In the first reported conviction for such an offence in more than 100 years, Graeme Raymond was yesterday found guilty in the Auckland District Court of having contributed to his insolvency by gambling, unjustifiable spending and extravagance in living."

Jo-Marie Brown and Anne Gibson – New Zealand journalists reporting this revealing story. In the sentencing the judge called it "riotous living at the upper end of the scale".

Lifestyle

"The high-flyer who loved his fast cars and was involved with numerous developments across Queensland had to move back in with his parents and his valuables were repossessed."

Kathy Sundstrom – Journalist reporting on Australian developer Scott Juniper.

Too funny (not for him), but like a true developer I believe he is making a comeback!

As Safe as Houses

"Million-dollar real estate agent claims
losing his Aston Martin
would cause 'extreme hardship'."

Amanda Saxton — journalist reporting on an Auckland real estate agent who had his driver's license suspended for speeding and drunk driving. The agent claimed he couldn't afford not to drive his Aston Martin Virage — as it was part of his "brand".

Lifestyle

"The developer's lifestyle is fantastic
— in between bankruptcies."

AJC

Many developers, at least the ones who did nothing illegal on their first plunge into liquidation, rise back to party once more.

As Safe as Houses

"I am an avid connoisseur of the life of luxury."

Emir Bahadir – As reported by Sarah Barns on the Turkish playboy whose parents own a billion-pound real estate empire. Emir's exploits include soaking up the sun with Lindsay Lohan and posing to the media on his luxury private jet.

Lifestyle

"When I built my first 10 houses,
people said I would go broke
and I've built thousands since.
I like to take risks."

Robert Campeau – A bombastic Canadian real estate developer whose luck did run out when he built a debt-fuelled department store empire in the United States, including Bloomingdale's, only for it to swiftly collapse in the frenzied financial climate of the 1980s.

As Safe as Houses

> "Rich people only like
> being around rich people.
> Nobody likes being around poor people,
> especially poor people."

Steve Wynn
Famously put his elbow through *Le Rêve*, a painting of Pablo Picasso's mistress Marie-Thérèse Walter, after he had conditionally sold it. Needless to say, the deal fell through. However, seven years later in 2013 he sold the restored painting to the same buyer for $155 million, $16 million more than the originally agreed sale price.

Lifestyle

"His 2008 'Best Damn Super Bowl Party' blew his previous parties away… The merrymaking included Playboy playmate Jenny McCarthy, Luda-cris, and comedian Chris Rock, as well as a swimsuit/lingerie fashion show, open bar and 'over-the-top opulence'…

The party was so loud and drew so many revellers that, by the third night, about 50 of Coles' neighbours demanded to meet with him about the ruckus."

John Dickerson – Phoenix reporter on the story of Scott Coles, an aggressive development financier (I can personally vouch for that from our limited dealings), who later took his own life. The company his father created and had conservatively run, failed at the beginning of the global financial crisis.

Chapter Eight

Leadership

Whether you are selling house, developing office buildings, designing apartments or building hospitals, the real property industry depends on decisions. With millions of dollars at stake in an uncertain environment, decision makers must make unwavering judgement calls to keep projects on track. For some — the plebs who consult — they merely defer the difficult calls up the food chain. The buck typically stops at the asset owner, developer, main contractor or (in times of trouble) the bank's front door. For them, firm leadership is essential.

The broad range of people in real estate also requires unsurpassed emotional intelligence to achieve results from concept through to delivery. Where else can you spend equal time convincing three-piece suited bankers to part with millions, as well as directing a burly salt of the earth brick layer building a wall, and restraining skyrocketing Italian marble costs proffered by impassioned right brain dominant interior designers?

Energy, tenacity, salesmanship, vision and a tough minded whatever-it-takes character are hallmarks of the world's most successful real estate leaders.

As Safe as Houses

"The basic principle is I command,
and my employees carry it out immediately."

Wang Jianlin
I haven't read that one in any recent modern age books on leadership! But he is the billionaire…

Leadership

"A sunny disposition is worth more than fortune."

Andrew Carnegie
Or kill 'em with love. In the real estate business a 'sunny disposition' often masks a 'smiling assassin'.

As Safe as Houses

"Ideas are cheap.
The difficult part is finding
the team to execute them."

Raymond Kwok – Hong Kong based billionaire real estate developer. With brothers Walter and Thomas they ran Sun Hung Kai Properties, builder of many of the iconic skyscrapers that define Hong Kong's skyline — until Thomas was convicted for corruption and sentenced to five years in prison.

Leadership

"A new CEO comes on board, they restructure.
Intellectual property gets sent out the door.

New general managers result,
they feel threatened or are simply required to change
and more IP is walked out the door.

Their reports restructure and
everyone remaining loses interest.

Can the last IP out,
please turn off the light."

AJC

On government departments' leadership incessant restructuring, where the only thing that actually happens is the intellectual property leaves the enterprise and everyone has to start again — to repeat the same mistakes and uncover the same realities.

As Safe as Houses

> "Do not plan for ventures before finishing what's at hand."

Euripides – Ancient Greek playwright.

Some developers flagrantly move onto the next project as soon as the fun (design + obtain financing) with the current one is done, but well before the project (or any profitability) is complete. They are always in search of the bigger deal. It is the lack of oversight over the detail of the projects already in progress that can be their downfall.

Leadership

"I'm easy. Very easy.

I'll tell you why I am easy.

If someone is no good, I get rid of them.

It is no good being tough

on somebody who can't do the job.

If he can do the job then

there is no point in being tough with him."

Harry Triguboff

Not afraid of colorfully telling it like he sees it, the *Daily Telegraph* reported him as saying, "The approvals process in Sydney is a disaster, it's been a disaster for many years. For me to get approval for excavation in Surfers Paradise takes one week, here maybe two years — that's hooliganism and it has to stop."

As Safe as Houses

"Management equals perspiration
Leadership equals inspiration."

"Management is about hiding
your emotions from others.
Leadership is about creating
emotions in others."

AJC
I have a lot to learn in the field of so-called leadership. Really, it's not like leading or commanding people into battle, but more like off-loading some positivity and vision to help get the team from where you are to where you want to be.

Leadership

"Without constantly pushing my
senior colleagues to formulate decisions,
I would never be able to learn and
know what they are made of."

Peter Woo – Billionaire businessman (inherited a real estate and shipping conglomerate from his father) and a significant real estate developer operating in Hong Kong, China and Singapore.

As Safe as Houses

"Blue sky thinking."

"Back to first principles."

Not said by AJC
Gibberish communicated to me in various corporate and government forums. Basically they mean what to do when we don't know how to develop a property and need to start thinking all over again.

Leadership

"Plans are only good intentions unless they immediately degenerate into hard work."

Peter Drucker – A business management guru. Tom Peters, the co-author of *In Search of Excellence*, called Drucker "the creator and inventor of modern management".

Action makes money in real estate, not plans. Also books are hard work (currently on my final edit, I hope!).

As Safe as Houses

"Eventually I just get them to construct
a feaso on the whiteboard."

AJC
The quick way to determine if a candidate is development manager material or merely a project manager, whilst building up new development teams. (Feaso also known as a financial feasibility or proforma.)

Leadership

"I think a good leader leads by example.
They must also be committed,
work with passion,
and won't say no to any good ideas,
no matter where they come from."

Ng Yek Meng – Managing Director, Progressive Builders, Singapore.

If it isn't working then you try something new. This is the best time to say yes to a team member's idea. Get them to drive the implementation. Even if it's a failure, (remember you were already on the back foot), they will be empowered to search for successful ideas next time.
That's why I came up with IDEAS. *I*nitiate, *D*ebate, *E*xperiment, *A*ction, and then once you have done it *S*urvey the results.

As Safe as Houses

"Management is about calling meetings.
Leadership is about preventing them."

AJC

I am not a fan of meetings. The very worst are when the meeting results in a plan to make a plan (aka in the government). What I do like are NASA style mission control centers where everyone is privy to commands and decisions in real time — without having to call a meeting!

Leadership

"Getting things done is critical and often
a hallmark of successful people.
There are two well known adages in this respect,
which I've certainly found to be correct.
First; do it now,
and second; if you want something done
then give it to a busy person."

Sir Bob Jones
I couldn't agree with you more, Mr Jones!

As Safe as Houses

"What separates the winners from the losers
is how a person reacts to each new twist of fate."

Donald Trump
Hasn't he had to deal with a few twists of fate? As I am writing, North Korea just launched another missile over Japan.

Leadership

> "Beware the rainmaker
> who can make it rain
> but can't collect the water."

AJC

I'm talking about those go getters and deal makers who believe they are visionary and certainly talk up a good spiel selling an opportunity. However, this group is the one that gloss over how they are going to deliver (profitably) on their promise, and ultimately fail time and time again — taking others' and their money with them.

As Safe as Houses

"Continuous, unflagging effort,
persistence and determination will win.
Let not the man be discouraged who has these."

James Whitcomb Riley – American poet and bestselling writer around the turn of the nineteenth century.

This sure does sum up the leadership qualities a real estate developer, or any entrepreneur for that matter, must summon in themselves.

Leadership

"It's about time we started using
a watch instead of a calendar."

AJC
The recipient wasn't so happy with this comment when my frustration at how long something was taking boiled over. Maybe I didn't appreciate everything else they had to do…Not!

As Safe as Houses

"I like thinking big.
To me it's very simple:
if you're going to be thinking anyway,
you might as well think big."

Donald Trump
Good point Donald. Many have said something similar in the ilk of "Aim for the stars hit the trees, aim for the trees hit the ground" — we get it!

Leadership

"Breaking through the GLASSE ceiling:

Growth =

Leadership +

Action +

Strategy X

Sales X

Everyone in the business."

AJC
My attempt at a corporate initialism.

Epilogue

Well that's what he said, that's what she said and that's what I said! With that now off my chest, it's time to go back and do some real (estate) work.

As Safe as Houses

Dad: "What do I do for work?"

Penelope (Age 3): "Talk to someone on the phone."

Dad: "What do I talk about?"

Penelope: "Talk to people so they can live…"

Dad: "How?"

Penelope: "Help people build the house…help hammer the house…put the roof on…then hammer the door.

Penelope: "Daddy."

Dad: "Yes?"

Penelope "Dad, Dad, the house needs windows too."

Dad: "Yes."

Penelope: "You make huts for lots of adults as well."

Dad: "Well I guess I do!"

References

http://www.phrases.org.uk/meanings/as-safe-as-houses.html

www.brainyquote.com

http://www.goodreads.com/quotes/tag/real-estate

https://www.realtymogul.com/resource-center/articles/20-famous-real-estate-investing-quotes

https://www.cbsnews.com/news/time-to-buy-a-home-now-says-barbara-corcoran/

http://quotesgram.com/raymond-kwok-quotes/

http://articles.latimes.com/1990-04-08/entertainment/ca-1646_1_american-comedian

https://www.planacademy.com/quotes-construction-building/

Potter, D. Sidney. (2017). *The Essayist: Reflections from a Real Estate Survivor: A Collection of Essays from The Huffington Post, Dissident Voice and CounterPunch.com* Bloomington: AuthorHouse

https://books.google.co.nz/books?id=aKlbDgAAQBAJ

https://books.google.co.nz/books?id=anUI5vdLyaEC

http://www.cebu-properties.net/resources/famous-real-estate-quotes-and-sayings/

References

https://www.huffingtonpost.com/entry/get-outside-the-real-estate-investment-box_us_59b2df0ee4b0c50640cd66f8

Trump, Donald. (2004). *Trump: The Way to the Top: The Best Business Advice I Ever Received.* New York: Crown Business.

http://www.quoteswise.com/bob-jones-quotes-2.html

http://9dailyquotes.com/quote/513327

http://www.isqft.com/start/blog-9-quotes-construction-inspire/

https://www.brandconstructors.com/great-construction-quotes/

https://www.planacademy.com/quotes-construction-building/

http://www.quotes.euronews.com/people/richard-lefrak-Nxb2qG2x

https://www.agentimage.com/blog/famous-quotes-about-real-estate/

https://userexperiences.co/10-great-quotes-for-user-experience-designers-972158b33936

http://edition.cnn.com/2005/US/10/31/real.estate.game/index.html

http://www.quoteswise.com

http://classics.mit.edu/Plato/laws.10.x.html

https://www.forbes.com/quotes/5443/

http://www.pbs.org/mormons/interviews/hinckley.html

http://izquotes.com/author/simon-reuben

http://www.berkshirehathaway.com/2001ar/2001letter.html

http://www.sgmoneymatters.com/what-does-billionaire-philip-ng-say-about-wealth/

As Safe as Houses

November 1966, *Changing Times—The Kiplinger Magazine*, "Notes on these changing times," pg. 2, col. 1. The Kiplinger Washington Editors.

https://books.google.co.nz/books?id=KAcEAAAAMBAJ

http://thinkexist.com/quotes/joseph_lau/

https://www.proudstories.com/joseph-lau-quotes.html

https://www.quotesdragon.com/joseph-lau-quotes/

http://www.azquotes.com/author/71015-Wang_Jianlin

https://www.inspiringquotes.us/author/9688-donald-bren

https://www.forbes.com/pictures/emeg45ikld/gerald-cavendish-grosvenor/#7a418d6d94b7

https://www.lwolf.com/blog/10-amazing-real-estate-quotes-inspire-you

https://www.forbes.com/sites/investor/2014/04/28/5-rules-of-contrarian-investing/

https://www.brainyquote.com/quotes/authors/w/wang_jianlin.html

https://books.google.co.nz/books?id=LbMwDwAAQBAJ

https://www.agentimage.com/blog/famous-quotes-about-real-estate/

http://www.woopidoo.com/business_quotes/real-estate.htm

https://www.brandconstructors.com/great-construction-quotes/

http://fitsmallbusiness.com/real-estate-quotes/

http://www.art-quotes.com/getquotes.php?catid=58#.WX_9y1UjGUl

http://www.wiseoldsayings.com/construction-quotes/

References

http://www.projectauditors.com/Company/Construction_Project_Management_Quotes_3.php

https://todayinsci.com/QuotationsCategories/C_Cat/Construction-Quotations.htm

https://www.workflowmax.com/blog/architecture/top-101-exceptionally-badass-quotes-architecture-design-legends

http://www.notable-quotes.com/a/architecture_quotes.html

https://www.biggerpockets.com/renewsblog/2012/12/30/motivational-quotes/

https://www.britannica.com/biography/Georg-Christoph-Lichtenberg

https://www.ft.com/content/28e22386-a11c-11e6-891e-abe238dee8e2

http://fortune.com/2015/07/09/china-skyscraper/

https://en.wikipedia.org/wiki/Harry_Triguboff

http://www.barbaracorcoran.com/

https://www.entrepreneur.com/article/250926

http://fortune.com/2013/05/23/barbara-corcoran-from-waitress-to-real-estate-queen/

https://www.npr.org/templates/transcript/transcript.php?storyId=525083696

https://en.wikipedia.org/wiki/Yakov_Smirnoff

https://www.forbes.com/profile/jeff-greene/

https://en.wikipedia.org/wiki/Jeff_Greene

https://www.forbes.com/global/2008/1013/096.html#748e2cfec462

https://www.richdadcoaching.com/

http://www.bravotv.com/million-dollar-listing-new-york/photos/the-tao-of-fredrik-eklund/item/9892901

http://www.richdad.com/Resources/Articles/booms-busts-and-where-opportunities-occur.aspx

https://en.wikipedia.org/wiki/Ray_Brown_(musician)

https://www.propertyobserver.com.au/finding/residential-investment/20144-tuesday-news-stick-to-bricks-and-mortar-harry-triguboffs-advice-to-investors-as-he-prepares-for-busy-50th-year-in-property-game.html

http://www.egizell.com/

http://www.nreionline.com/international/zell-talks-politics-debt-international-markets-and-how-hes-investing-today

https://www.ft.com/content/ea9f603c-33e9-11e7-99bd-13beb0903fa3

http://iloverealestate.tv/triguboffs-golden-rule-of-property/

https://www.stratalive.com.au/2010/03/02/harrys_trigonometry

http://www.nytimes.com/2008/10/17/opinion/17buffett.html

http://www.reubenfoundation.com/brothers-reuben-lifestyles-magazine/

http://www.thecompletesalespersoncourse.com.au/article/barbara-corcoran-pick-of-the-litter

https://www.forbes.com/sites/joshhelmin/2010/09/29/urgent-advice-from-billionaire-john-paulson-buy-a-house-and-gold-plus-rupert-murdochs-pay-cut/#7c9c4a40f183

https://www.forbes.com/sites/robertlenzner/2010/09/27/john-paulson-sell-bonds-buy-stocks-double-digit-inflation-coming/#1ffd7cfb468c

http://mark.markrubinstein-author.com/am-i-being-too-subtle-a-talk-with-sam-zell/

References

https://books.google.co.nz/books?id=7Q3rDQAAQBAJ&pg=PT161&lpg=PT161&dq=design+isn't+finished+Brenda+Laurel#

https://www.newyorker.com/magazine/2007/11/12/rough-rider

http://rjholdings.co.nz/

https://www.forbes.com/profile/steve-wynn/

http://www.sarahbeeny.com/

https://www.penguinrandomhouse.com/books/318899/am-i-being-too-subtle-by-sam-zell/9781591848233/

https://www.forbes.com/profile/sam-zell/

https://www.forbes.com/profile/stephen-ross/

https://en.wikipedia.org/wiki/Anderson_Cooper

http://www.morningstar.in/posts/34128/1/investing-lessons-from-a-%22professional-opportunist%22.aspx

https://www.biography.com/people/andrew-carnegie-9238756

https://www.donaldjtrump.com/

http://dcgoldberg.blogspot.co.nz/2009/02/harry-in-hurry-bulletin-111207.html

http://au.phaidon.com/agenda/architecture/articles/2014/april/02/what-did-mies-van-der-rohe-mean-by-less-is-more/

https://en.wikipedia.org/wiki/Will_Rogers

http://fawnrogers.com/frank-gehry/

https://quoteinvestigator.com/2011/05/03/architect-vines/

https://books.google.co.nz/books?id=d5ikDAAAQBAJ&pg=PA201&l

https://www.biography.com/people/franklin-d-roosevelt-9463381

As Safe as Houses

https://www.forbes.com/profile/david-simon-reuben/

http://www.nytimes.com/1999/06/21/nyregion/louis-j-glickman-94-investor-linked-to-carnegie-hall-deal.html

https://www.forbes.com/profile/john-paulson/

https://books.google.co.nz/books?id=vv3dT-kyuu8C&pg=PA19&lpg=PA19

http://www.history.com/topics/john-d-rockefeller

https://www.britannica.com/biography/Winston-Churchill

https://en.wikipedia.org/wiki/Gordon_B._Hinckley

http://www.nytimes.com/learning/general/onthisday/bday/1215.html

https://therealdeal.com/issues_articles/william-levitt-the-king-of-suburbia/

http://www.nytimes.com/1994/01/29/obituaries/william-j-levitt-86-pioneer-of-suburbs-dies.html?pagewanted=all

https://www.britannica.com/biography/Jorge-Luis-Borges

https://www.brainyquote.com/quotes/authors/l/leo_aikman.html

https://en.wikipedia.org/wiki/Jeff_Davidson

http://www.iep.utm.edu/plato/

https://www.britannica.com/biography/John-Ruskin

https://plato.stanford.edu/entries/nietzsche/

http://www.telegraph.co.uk/news/obituaries/1482161/Philip-Johnson.html

https://www.coupland.com/about

https://therealdeal.com/tag/richard-mack/

https://todayinsci.com/H/Hood_William/HoodWilliam-Quotations.htm

References

https://www.biography.com/people/frank-gehry-9308278

http://miessociety.org/mies/projects/

http://www.ramsa.com/

https://en.wikipedia.org/wiki/Robert_A._M._Stern

http://www.pritzkerprize.com/biography-philip-johnson

https://www.biography.com/people/frank-lloyd-wright-9537511

http://franklloydwright.org/

http://www.toureiffel.paris/en/all-about-the-eiffel-tower/history-and-figures-about-the-eiffel-tower/gustave-eiffel

https://en.wikipedia.org/wiki/Brenda_Laurel

http://www.designishistory.com/1960/massimo-vignelli/

https://www.biography.com/people/louis-kahn-37884

http://libeskind.com/people/daniel-libeskind/

http://thegreatdiscontent.com/interview/frank-chimero

https://en.wikipedia.org/wiki/Peter_Cook_(architect)

https://nl.wikipedia.org/wiki/Mieke_Gerritzen

http://pcparch.com/firm/people/cesar-pelli-faia

http://www.independent.co.uk/arts-entertainment/architecture/zaha-hadid-google-doodle-buildings-celebration-architecture-qatar-london-stadiums-centres-a7764071.html

http://www.independent.co.uk/arts-entertainment/architecture/frank-gehry-dont-call-me-a-starchitect-1842870.html

https://books.google.co.nz/books?id=8OOwn_KzkmIC&pg=PA54&lpg=PA54

https://www.collectionscanada.gc.ca/confederation/023001-4000.39-e.html

https://www.britannica.com/biography/Johann-Wolfgang-von-Goethe

https://americanliterature.com/author/ambrose-bierce/bio-books-stories

http://www.fosterandpartners.com/about-us/team/senior-executive-partners/norman-foster/

https://en.wikipedia.org/wiki/Norman_Foster,_Baron_Foster_of_Thames_Bank

https://www.biography.com/people/le-corbusier-9376609

https://www.britannica.com/biography/Le-Corbusier

http://www.pritzkerprize.com/2001/bio

https://www.bauhaus100.de/en/past/people/directors/walter-gropius/

https://www.britannica.com/biography/Walter-Gropius

https://www.forbes.com/profile/lee-shau-kee/

https://en.wikipedia.org/wiki/Lee_Shau-kee

https://www.forbes.com/profile/wang-jianlin/

https://en.wikipedia.org/wiki/Wang_Jianlin

https://en.wikipedia.org/wiki/Donald_Bren

https://www.forbes.com/profile/donald-bren/

http://www.notablebiographies.com/Co-Da/Coward-Noel.html

https://www.noelcoward.com/

http://www.sgmoneymatters.com/what-does-billionaire-philip-ng-say-about-wealth/

https://www.forbes.com/profile/robert-philip-ng/

References

https://www.thesun.co.uk/news/3004082/danny-lambo-millionaire-pavilion-hotel-howd-you-get-so-rich/

http://www.independent.co.uk/news/world/asia/antics-of-the-capital-playboys-disgust-china-2358185.html

https://www.irishtimes.com/news/playboy-of-the-eastern-world-faces-charges-after-late-night-showdown-1.605149

http://www.seattlepi.com/local/article/Indictment-Seattle-banker-lived-lavish-lifestyle-1456600.php

http://www.nzherald.co.nz/nz/news/article.cfm?c_id=1&objectid=188271

https://www.sunshinecoastdaily.com.au/news/i-lost-it-all-scott-juniper-reveals-battle-to-reco/3117852/

http://www.stuff.co.nz/national/crime/89800380/Million-dollar-real-estate-agent-claims-losing-his-Aston-Martin-would-cause-extreme-hardship

https://www.thesun.co.uk/living/4198043/turkish-playboy-emir-bahadir-whose-parents-own-a-billion-pound-real-estate-empire-soaks-up-the-sun-with-lindsay-lohan-and-poses-for-pics-on-his-luxury-private-jet/

https://www.nytimes.com/2017/06/21/business/obituary-robert-campeau-dead-bloomingdales.html

http://www.phoenixnewtimes.com/news/scott-coles-the-story-behind-the-life-and-death-of-the-flamboyant-owner-of-mortgages-ltd-6450264

http://www.ancient-literature.com/greece_euripides.html

https://www.forbes.com/profile/thomas-raymond-kwok/

https://www.forbes.com/profile/peter-woo/

https://www.forbes.com/lists/2006/10/VFSP.html

http://www.drucker.institute/about-peter-f-drucker/

https://www.poetryfoundation.org/poets/james-whitcomb-riley

https://www.biography.com/people/antoni-gaud%C3%AD-40695

https://www.casabatllo.es/en/antoni-gaudi/

http://www.nytimes.com/2007/11/07/us/07mit.html

https://en.wikipedia.org/wiki/Ludwig_Mies_van_der_Rohe

http://www.theartstory.org/movement-bauhaus.htm

https://en.wikipedia.org/wiki/Barcelona_chair

http://franklloydwright.org/

https://www.fallingwater.org/

http://www.designcurial.com/news/louis-kahn---six-most-important-buildings-4323752/

https://web.archive.org/web/20110610221849/http://www.cnbc.com/id/23407363/Real_Estate_Mogul_Jeff_Greene_The_Man_Who_Shorted_Subprime

http://www.archdaily.com/334095/happy-112th-birthday-louis-kahn

https://www.dezeen.com/tag/daniel-libeskind/

http://www.architecturaldigest.com/gallery/daniel-libeskind-architecture/all

http://libeskind.com/people/daniel-libeskind/

https://www.austria.info/au/activities/culture-traditions/museums-in-austria/kunsthaus-graz

https://en.wikipedia.org/wiki/Petronas_Towers

https://www.petronastwintowers.com.my/

http://www.telegraph.co.uk/travel/galleries/zaha-hadid-unfinished-buildings/

References

http://www.pritzkerprize.com/laureates/year

http://1000museum.com/

http://www.telegraph.co.uk/finance/newsbysector/constructionandproperty/11222188/13-things-you-didnt-know-about-the-Gherkin.html

http://www.villa-savoye.fr/en/

https://www.dezeen.com/2016/07/24/le-corbusier-notre-dame-du-haut-ronchamp-chapel-france-unesco-world-heritage-list/

https://placesjournal.org/article/an-interview-with-jacques-herzog

https://www.iconeye.com/architecture/features/item/12481-jacques-herzog-i-think-we-have-a-certain-social-responsibility

http://www.tate.org.uk/about/projects/tate-modern-project

https://en.wikipedia.org/wiki/Beijing_National_Stadium

http://www.npr.org/sections/thetwo-way/2013/03/26/175412881/years-after-the-elbow-incident-steve-wynn-sells-picassos-le-r-ve-for-155-million

http://www.scmp.com/news/hong-kong/economy/article/1864594/hong-kong-tycoon-lee-shau-kee-hands-out-hk15-million-birth

http://www.businessinsider.com/donald-bren-profile-2016-2

http://www.npr.org/sections/thetwo-way/2013/03/26/175412881/years-after-the-elbow-incident-steve-wynn-sells-picassos-le-r-ve-for-155-million

https://www.forbes.com/sites/luisakroll/2014/12/19/hong-kong-billionaire-thomas-kwok-found-guilty-brother-raymond-not-guilty/#46e3c93722fc

As Safe as Houses

https://www.ft.com/content/ea9f603c-33e9-11e7-99bd-13beb0903fa3

http://www.theaustralian.com.au/business/opinion/robert-gottliebsen/how-harry-triguboff-climbed-his-way-to-the-top/news-story/d67503509defb03efda0bf1a093c9f1c

http://www.theaustralian.com.au/business/property/harry-triguboff-blasts-party-leaders-lack-of-vision/news-story/32c1e17a86765f0db40d84d6425de1d6

http://www.dailytelegraph.com.au/news/nsw/billionaire-harry-triguboff-slams-sydneys-planning-hooliganism-for-delaying-building-of-new-homes/news-story/47a44949c8c45f477a23a63dcec26cd9

https://successstory.com/people/harry-oscar-triguboff-ao

https://www.theurbandeveloper.com/meriton-harry-triguboff-apartment-portfolio/

http://penguin.co.nz/authors/37-bob-jones

http://www.noted.co.nz/money/investment/sir-bob-jones-on-how-we-get-it-wrong-with-saving/

http://www.stuff.co.nz/entertainment/3647766/Multimillionaire-tells-off-the-apprentice

http://www.getfrank.co.nz/editorial/features/the-actual-habits-sir-bobjones

http://www.scoop.co.nz/stories/HL0509/S00091.htm

http://www.firstpost.com/business/seven-interesting-facts-about-mumbai-born-reuben-brothers-who-saved-sahara-2284418.html

http://www.nytimes.com/1999/06/21/nyregion/louis-j-glickman-94-investor-linked-to-carnegie-hall-deal.html?mcubz=3

References

https://www.forbes.com/sites/bisnow/2017/03/21/the-rockefeller-dynastys-most-prestigious-real-estate/#7cf2175569d0

https://www.forbes.com/sites/investor/2014/04/28/5-rules-of-contrarian-investing/#6f297423c360

https://www.thebalance.com/how-sam-zell-became-a-real-estate-mogul-4046199

https://www.valuewalk.com/2017/06/sam-zell-am-i-being-too-subtle-a-negotiation-win/

https://www.mansionglobal.com/articles/42906-winston-churchill-s-historic-london-home-listed-for-36-million

https://www.fastcodesign.com/3053937/9-things-you-didnt-know-about-frank-gehry

https://www.theguardian.com/artanddesign/2014/oct/24/frank-gehry-journalist-finger-architecture-shit

https://www.vanityfair.com/culture/2015/09/why-frank-gehry-is-not-a-starchitect

http://www.archdaily.com/784297/20-things-you-didnt-know-about-mies-van-der-rohe

https://www.theguardian.com/artanddesign/2002/nov/30/architecture.artsfeatures

https://www.architecturaldigest.com/frank-lloyd-wright

https://www.architecturaldigest.com/frank-lloyd-wright

http://flwright.org/aboutus/wright150

http://untappedcities.com/2017/04/21/10-frank-lloyd-wright-buildings-in-and-around-nyc/

http://untappedcities.com/2017/04/21/10-frank-lloyd-wright-buildings-in-and-around-nyc/

https://www.theguardian.com/artanddesign/2017/may/21/frank-lloyd-wright-fantasist-or-genius-exhibition-moma-new-york

https://www.mprnews.org/story/2007/01/19/flwrightprofile

http://freshome.com/2012/09/03/10-great-architectural-lessons-from-frank-lloyd-wright/

http://www.businessinsider.com/what-frank-lloyd-wright-got-wrong-2016-8/?r=AU&IR=T

http://www.independent.co.uk/arts-entertainment/architecture/architect-of-desire-frank-lloyd-wrights-private-life-was-even-more-unforgettable-than-his-buildings-1637537.html

http://franklloydwrightsites.com/arizona/biltmore/biltmore.html

http://www.americaslibrary.gov/aa/carnegie/aa_carnegie_phil_1.html

http://www.americaslibrary.gov/aa/carnegie/aa_carnegie_phil_1.html

http://library.columbia.edu/locations/rbml/units/carnegie/andrew.html

http://www.inspireux.com/2008/04/09/the-life-of-a-designer-is-a-life-of-fight-against-the-ugliness/

https://www.youtube.com/watch?v=9g3Ogtgleyg

http://papers.cumincad.org/data/works/att/1b31.content.03079.pdf

https://books.google.co.nz/books?id=jAiUBwAAQBAJ&pg=PA88&lpg=PA88#v=onepage&q&f=false

https://twitter.com/aianational/status/299978544648441856?lang=en

References

https://www.architectural-review.com/rethink/reputations-pen-portraits-/daniel-libeskind-1946-/8620025.article

https://www.moma.org/documents/moma_press-release_325576.pdf

http://www.arabianbusiness.com/changing-fortunes-damac-s-ziad-el-chaar-632274.html

http://www.nytimes.com/2001/09/19/nyregion/reaching-sky-finding-limit-tall-buildings-face-new-doubt-symbols-vulnerability.html

https://www.reuters.com/article/us-money-lifelessons-caruso/lessons-on-empire-building-from-real-estate-developer-rick-caruso-idUSKBN17F1LW

https://books.google.co.nz/books?id=7j8OomOrbgUC&pg=PA60

http://www.theceomagazine.com/business/ng-yek-meng/

https://www.theguardian.com/artanddesign/2007/oct/11/architecture

https://www.theglobeandmail.com/report-on-business/at-92-bc-billionaire-joseph-segal-is-still-hard-at-work/article35778043/

http://www.spiegel.de/international/world/spiegel-interview-with-chinese-billionaire-zhang-xin-a-1073417.html

https://twitter.com/realdonaldtrump/status/276692448661606401?lang=en

https://www.theguardian.com/sport/2015/aug/04/rio-olympic-games-2016-property-developer-carlos-carvalho-barra

http://www.ladowntownnews.com/news/geoff-palmer-speaks-out/article_83dd6790-79a0-11e5-9f2c-a3035a2d9db8.html

https://www.planningreport.com/2015/10/30/palmer-re-gentrified-downtown-la-despite-doubters-and-design-criticism

https://www.director.co.uk/7875-property-developer-sir-stuart-lipton-reveals-why-he-likes-to-upset-the-status-quo/

https://www.standard.co.uk/business/markets/sir-stuart-lipton-the-veteran-property-developer-with-a-vision-for-a-swathe-of-rundown-london-9920001.html

http://www.dailymail.co.uk/news/article-5065691/Resurrecting-London-s-ghost-town-Silvertown.html

http://people.com/archive/high-roller-vol-40-no-23/

http://www.nzherald.co.nz/nz/news/article.cfm?c_id=1&objectid=10859136

http://www.longbeachrepublicanwomen.com/contact.html

https://books.google.co.nz/books?id=doYzq9z-eosC&pg=PA41

http://www.theaustralian.com.au/life/home-design/just-wild-about-harry/news-story/61a3eff3822ef55bfd83f78d40ef6562

http://blogs.bakerhughes.com/reservoir/2015/07/07/dont-miss-the-unconventional-resource-revolutions-next-wave-part-22/

http://www.aolib.com/reader_17976_3.htm

http://www.telegraph.co.uk/news/worldnews/asia/china/10325019/The-rise-and-rise-of-Wang-Jianlin-Chinas-richest-man.html

https://www.asia.finance/lifestyle/rich-people-like-around-rich-people/

https://books.google.co.nz/books?id=JNQhDAAAQBAJ&pg=PT4

References

http://www.ocregister.com/2010/11/28/bren-talks-about-giving-away-money/

https://www.ft.com/content/2b2746c0-a663-11e1-9453-00144feabdc0

https://www.forbes.com/sites/russellflannery/2011/11/14/wealth-tips-from-one-of-asias-richest-entrepreneurs-lee-shau-kee/#6c9cac781cd1

https://books.google.co.nz/books?id=aiGewkGMBRgC&pg=PT299

https://books.google.co.nz/books?id=whg05Z4Nwo0C&pg=PA61

https://www.dezeen.com/2016/02/25/jacques-herzog-de-meuron-all-architecture-humanitarian-approach-blavatnik-school-government-university-of-oxford/

http://www.designers-books.com/towards-a-new-architecture-le-corbusier-1927/

http://articles.chicagotribune.com/2003-09-21/features/0309210347_1_le-corbusier-home-design-home-design

https://books.google.co.nz/books?id=iY-BAgAAQBAJ&pg=PA64

https://www.wsj.com/articles/SB116683600262058277

https://www.archdaily.com/777366/ted-talk-norman-foster-on-green-architecture

https://www.ted.com/talks/norman_foster_s_green_agenda

https://publicdomainreview.org/collections/the-cynics-word-book-1906/

https://books.google.co.nz/books?id=RmOn2T-35dcC&pg=PA56

As Safe as Houses

https://www.forbes.com/sites/yjeanmundelsalle/2015/06/01/pritzker-prize-winning-architect-zaha-hadids-crafts-designs-that-go-with-the-flow/2/#b76f1e61b14a

About the Author

Andrew Crosby has worked in real estate, primarily development, since the late nineties. With degrees in Architecture and Property from the University of Auckland he embarked on a corporate career in real estate consulting with Ernst & Young only to be drawn to a private property development company before his first year was done.

He has managed (and still does) projects ranging from residential subdivisions, terrace homes and apartments to mixed use, retail and office developments. This includes international experience in New Zealand, Australia and the United States and a senior management role with Housing New Zealand, where he led the property development team to initiate and deliver hundreds (eventually becoming thousands) of new homes in public-private ventures.

Looking at improving efficiency in the development process, Andrew founded an internet start-up in project collaboration that was used for large construction projects, including apartments, hospitals, wastewater and road networks, train stations, airports and prisons.

He also set up the inaugural management office of the Royal Institution of Chartered Surveyors in New Zealand – a general manager role that included co-producing the *RICS Development Monitoring Guide*.

Exemplifying a willingness to continuously learn, a personal highlight was attending a course in real estate development and finance at Massachusetts Institute of Technology in 2010.

As a part-time lecturer at Unitec, Auckland, New Zealand since 2014, Andrew delivers the Bachelor of Construction final year paper in property development.

Feel free to contact Andrew at

andrew.crosby@aenspire.com

or visit

www.developmentprofit.com

What's your quote?

Go on have a go!

www.ingramcontent.com/pod-product-compliance
Lightning Source LLC
Chambersburg PA
CBHW020649220526
45464CB00001B/356